and I would make eye contact, and I could tell just looking at him, the disbelief that here we were, a year after starting to work on the script, and here the actual actors were, speaking these lines that he and Larry had written with these iconic characters coming to life. There were just certain moments where it was an out-of-body experience. It was like, 'How did we end up here? And why are Kathy Kennedy and Lucasfilm and Disney crazy enough to allow us to make this movie?'"
—Bryan Burk, producer

An Introduction...

Star Wars is many things. At the core, it's this family saga. It's a family drama. It is about finding your own strength and finding connections with people you wouldn't anticipate knowing. It's about secrets and causes and joining something larger than yourself. Good and evil. At the core of it, there are characters that you love. Characters that make you laugh and make you care. There's this authenticity in *Star Wars: A New Hope* and *The Empire Strikes Back* and *Return of the Jedi* where you're feeling this wonderful family, even though they're not related. It's a family of underdogs working together. It's such a powerful feeling. We all want to feel that if things got desperate, we'd run into someone who we'd instantly love, whether we love them in a brotherly, sisterly way or something else. There's a feeling of the world that it is full of allies that you might run into to help in the fight against a villain that you might not otherwise be able to confront.

While there was never a doubt that the visual opportunities were enormous—the worlds we'd travel to, the creatures we'd meet, the weapons and ships and landscapes—none of that matters if you don't love the people in the ships or if you don't love the people who are choosing to fight, or in some cases run from. So, the core of this story had to be what makes any story work—the characters. The fundamental thing that Lawrence Kasdan and I were focusing on was how to make these characters people that we immediately care about and at least are intrigued by. How do we make them have choices and have behavior that we pull back, or raise questions about them that we want to understand? It was the thing that was most important for us in the process. We wanted to find characters that we wanted to watch in a story. We knew there would be no shortage of obstacles, challenges and evil to throw in their path.

 **–J.J. ABRAMS**

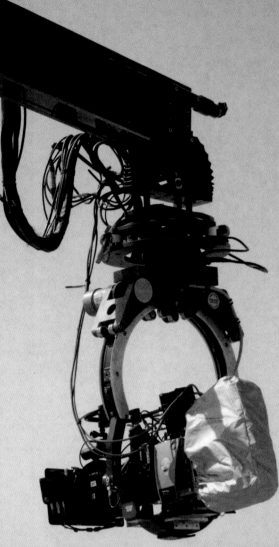

INSIDE

John Boyega as Finn
on location in Abu
Dhabi. "Going out
there and being in this
environment—huge
desert, loads of props,
a big set and obviously
J.J. Abrams with his
enthusiasm and his
energy, coming in
and saying that we're
starting *Star Wars*
Episode VII—was just
amazing," Boyega says.
"I knew it was going to
be an experience I will
never forget."

A Long Time Ago....

EPISODE I

The Trade Federation institutes a blockade around the planet Naboo in response to the planet's opposition to taxation in the Galactic Republic. The blockade is secretly run by the Sith Order, who are hoping to undermine the Republic. Supreme Chancellor Valorum sends Jedi Master Qui-Gon Jinn and his apprentice, Obi-Wan Kenobi, to Naboo to negotiate with the Trade Federation. Surprised by the Jedi, the Federation launches an attack on Naboo.

Rescuing the Queen of Naboo, the young Padmé Amidala, as the Federation is about to force her to sign a treaty making their invasion legal, Qui-Gon and Obi-Wan flee with her, intending to get to Coruscant and the Galactic Senate. The fleeing Jedi and Queen Amidala are forced to land on the planet Tatooine. There, they find a 9-year-old slave, Anakin Skywalker, who Qui-Gon believes may be the "Chosen One" and determines to train him as a Jedi.

On Coruscant, Qui-Gon lobbies for Anakin to be accepted as a Jedi apprentice, but the masters of the Order feel the boy is susceptible to the dark side of the Force and initially refuse. Qui-Gon takes it upon himself to train Anakin. The Jedi Council is forced to consider the possible return of the Sith.

Senator Palpatine is nominated as new Chancellor. During the Battle of Naboo, in which Amidala's troops and an army of native Gungans fight the Federation's droids, Qui-Gon Jinn is killed in a lightsaber battle with Darth Maul, apprentice to Darth Sidious, a Sith Lord orchestrating the downfall of the Galactic Republic. Obi-Wan Kenobi takes on the training of Anakin Skywalker.

EPISODE II

A decade after the Battle for Naboo, a former Jedi Master named Count Dooku consolidates a separatist movement that threatens the Republic. Padmé Amidala, now a senator representing Naboo, narrowly survives an attempt on her life and is placed under the protection of Obi-Wan Kenobi and Anakin Skywalker.

Obi-Wan Kenobi travels to the planet Kamino, where he discovers an army of clones genetically based on bounty hunter Jango Fett has been built for the Republic. Meanwhile, as his relationship with Padmé blossoms, Anakin Skywalker suffers from visions of his mother so intense he travels to Tatooine to save her. When he finds her near death in the camp of some Tusken Raiders, he succumbs to anger and kills them all.

TRACKING THE MAJOR MOMENTS IN THE *STAR WARS* SAGA
THAT LED TO *THE FORCE AWAKENS*.

The Jedi council learns from Obi-Wan that Count Dooku is building a Separatist droid army with the help of the Trade Federation. To combat this threat, Supreme Chancellor Palpatine is granted emergency powers, which he uses to send the clone troopers into battle against the Separatists, marking the beginning of the Clone Wars.

EPISODE III

At the Battle of Utapau, Obi-Wan Kenobi kills General Grievous, but the entire assault is a diversionary tactic by Chancellor Palpatine to separate Obi-Wan from Anakin and seduce the younger Jedi with the dark side of the Force. Anakin Skywalker discovers that Palpatine is really the Sith leader of the evil anti-Republic Confederacy.

● ● ●

Believing that the dark side is the only path to saving the life of his wife Padmé, Anakin Skywalker becomes Sidious's Sith apprentice, Darth Vader.

Chancellor Palpatine delivers Order 66, a tightly orchestrated command to have clone troops assassinate their Jedi generals.

● ● ●

On Mustafar, Obi-Wan Kenobi and Darth Vader battle, with Obi-Wan severely injuring and dismembering Vader, leaving him badly burned and near death. Meanwhile, Yoda and Palpatine fight to a stalemate on Coruscant, and Palpatine declares himself the first Galactic Emperor.

Obi-Wan brings Padmé safely to the asteroid Polis Massa, where she gives birth to twins, Luke and Leia, before dying. Luke is sent to Tatooine to live with Anakin's stepbrother Owen Lars and his wife, while Leia is adopted by Senator Bail Organa of Alderaan.

EPISODE IV

A generation later, Leia, now a Rebel leader, is intercepted by Imperial forces while in possession of plans to the Death Star, but she is able to embed the plans into R2-D2's memory before sending the droid to Tatooine in an escape pod along with C-3PO. There, the droids are eventually bought by Luke Skywalker. Luke follows the droids after R2-D2 runs away, eventually meeting his father's old Jedi Master.

Luke goes with Obi-Wan Kenobi to Mos Eisley, where the two hire the *Millennium Falcon* and its crew, Han Solo and Chewbacca, to take them to Alderaan, where they believe Leia to be. En route, the ship is apprehended and taken to the Death Star.

● ● ●

Rescuing Leia, Luke, Han and Chewbacca escape the Death Star with the droids after Obi-Wan sacrifices his life. But the ship carries a homing device that alerts the Empire to the Rebel position on Yavin 4.

In a daring attempt to destroy the Death Star before it can destroy their base, Rebels including Luke Skywalker take to their X- and Y-wing fighters in the Battle of Yavin. Luke uses the Force and is successful in destroying the space station.

EPISODE V

The Battle of Hoth costs countless Rebel lives as the new Rebel Base on the icy planet is overrun by Imperial troops. Han, Leia, Chewie and C-3PO escape aboard the *Millennium Falcon*, and Luke flees Hoth in his X-wing.

Luke travels to the Dagobah system to stu with Master Yoda and complete his training. Meanwhile, Darth Vade puts a bounty on the *Millennium Falcon*. Amo those who take him up the offer is Boba Fett, s of the clone-troop mod Jango Fett.

● ● ●

Han Solo—unaware tha Boba Fett is tracking him—makes his way to planet Bespin, where h friend Lando Calrissian in charge of Cloud City, mining colony. Lando is forced into a deal with Empire, and Han is froz in carbonite and hande over to Fett.

Luke arrives at Cloud City in time to confront Darth Vader, who reveals that he is Luke's father. He cuts off Luke's hand in battle. Luke escapes and is fitted with a robotic replacement hand after his rescue.

EPISODE VI

With his Jedi training nearly complete, Luke carries out an elaborate plan to rescue Han from Jabba's palace on Tatooine with the help of Leia, Lando, Chewbacca and the droids. During the ensuing melee, Leia kills Jabba the Hutt, and Boba Fett falls into the Sarlacc pit to be digested for 1,000 years.

The Rebel Alliance discovers that plans are underway to create a new Death Star and launch an attack on the station's shield generators on the forest moon of Endor.

Darth Vader takes Luke to the new Death Star in an attempt to get him to join the dark side. Luke refuses. Emperor Palpatine attempts to kill Luke, but Vader comes to his son's aid and kills Palpatine. He sacrifices his own life in the process.

As the Empire reels from the defeats of its Death Stars, the Rebel Alliance consolidates itself into the New Republic. The leaders of the struggling Empire plan a summit on Akiva to discuss the future of their regime.

EPISODE VII

Corruption and darkness infect the Galactic Senate. The First Order, a military and political organization inspired by the Galactic Empire, extends its sphere of influence. Supreme Leader Snoke aims for total domination.

Unwilling to let the First Order prevail, Leia leads a movement of freedom fighters: the Resistance. In need of Luke's help, she sends her best pilot, Poe Dameron, to the desert planet Jakku to recover a map that leads to her brother.

The First Order troops land on Jakku too, in search of the same map. Poe hides it in his droid, BB-8, which is later found by a young scavenger named Rey.

Together with Finn, a former stormtrooper who left the First Order, Rey and BB-8 leave Jakku. Their mission is to take the map to the Resistance, but they are pursued by a dark figure: Kylo Ren—a member of the mysterious Knights of Ren—who betrayed Luke Skywalker and who will stop at nothing to find him now.

Self-professed super fan Pablo Hidalgo safeguards the legacies of all the characters in the Star Wars Universe as part of the Lucasfilm story team.

Expert Analysis

PABLO HIDALGO, CREATIVE EXECUTIVE AND MEMBER OF THE LUCASFILM STORY TEAM, HELPS DEFINE BOTH THE *STAR WARS* CANON AS WELL AS THE NAMES OF THE CHARACTERS WHO EXIST WITHIN IT.

I ***n what ways did your job on the story team manifest itself in* The Force Awakens*?***
It started way back in early 2012 when there were some initial story meetings about what the shape of this first movie and potential subsequent movies would be. So at the time I dealt very much with Michael Arndt, who was the first screenwriter who was brought on board to take a look at Episode VII and develop that story. Michael really just looked to get information on the shape and political landscape of the *Star Wars* Universe, and also asked what had been done before in this space, mainly to see what could be learned from those earlier iterations. When J.J. Abrams and Lawrence Kasdan began working on the screenplay, a lot of it was more granular details; more questions about the function of the *Millennium Falcon*. Could a single character pilot it? If there was only a single person piloting it, what kind of shortcomings might that person have?

What sort of conversations did the story group have about the character of Luke Skywalker and what his role would be in* The Force Awakens*?
The books had Luke reestablish the Jedi Order to essentially mimic and mirror what we had known or what we came to discover about the prequel Jedi. And I understand how that impulse came about because as these stories were being told, that information was being revealed

Pablo Hidalgo is also the author of *The Visual Dictionary for Star Wars: The Force Awakens*, a comprehensive guide to the entire film. The book is available everywhere now.

through Episodes I, II and III—so all of sudden this new insight into the Jedi Order was being applied to what happened after *Return of the Jedi*. But chronologically, from a point of view in the universe, that doesn't necessarily make much sense. We know looking at it in order from Episodes I–VI that Luke would have the opportunity to look back at what had come before and make different decisions and come to realize the shortcomings of the Jedi Order, or at least be a little bit more thoughtful on what he was doing going forward. The other thing that came about was that Han and Leia basically become like a Washington, D.C. power couple in the books. They both get involved in politics. So ultimately what Michael Arndt had decided upon—and this was bolstered by George Lucas's instinct in terms of where he wanted the characters as well—is the books had Han and Leia be way too central in a position of power, and being that central didn't allow as much drama as the story demanded. It also made it difficult to bring new characters and a new generation of heroes into the fold.

How essential is it to have new characters as an entry point for this next generation of films?
It's absolutely essential because this is a new generation story and as much as we love the old generation, this is a place for new heroes and new villains to arise. And that's one of the things that 30 years of publishing did not do as well as it could have because Luke, Han and Leia were such marquee characters, so every time a problem arose in the galaxy it fell to them to solve it. As a result, you have these characters who have not been given a single rest over 30 years facing crisis after crisis. You never really had the torch-handing moment. These films accomplish that. Han, Luke and Leia got their trilogy and now it's time for folks like Finn, Poe and Rey to step forward. It's their chance to save the universe from whatever villainy might pop up.

This early look at the scavenger Rey by concept artists Yanick Dusseault and Iain McCaig (above) was created to give a sense of Rey's still-developing character and what vehicle she could use to traverse the wastelands of Jakku. Before landing on her final speeder design (below), artists had Rey piloting full-fledged starships as well as speeder bikes and landspeeders.

Daisy Ridley as **Rey**

YOUNG, **BOLD** and independent, Rey lives alone in the desert on the remote planet of Jakku. As a scavenger, she spends her days exploring a spaceship graveyard and the enormous vessels abandoned there. She removes valuable parts and pieces of technology, then sells them for food at Niima Outpost. One day, Rey saves a small droid from another scavenger: The droid is called BB-8, and it has a secret mission to accomplish. Helping BB-8, Rey begins a journey that will take her a long way from Jakku and from who she had always thought she was.

How did you hear about the part?
The first time I actually heard about this I was with three friends. One is a makeup artist and the other is a stylist. Somebody said, "Did you hear *Star Wars* is coming out?" I immediately emailed my agent and said that I really need to be seen for this. I don't know why; I just had this weird feeling. I wound up getting an audition. So, for the first audition I was an hour early. Literally pacing up and down outside. I'd never been nervous like that before for something. It was the first time in an audition process that I felt everyone was rooting, not for me, but for the idea of an unknown person getting the part.

How did you find out you got the part?
My last audition was really amazing. A few days later, I knew I'd hear from J.J., and my phone was broken. I didn't get the call. I didn't know what was going on. I finally got through to him, and he told me I'd be starring in *Star Wars*.

Who is Rey, and what is her role in the story?
Rey begins in her own world. She goes on this crazy adventure and meets Finn and BB-8, and she finally starts to make these bonds she's never had before.

Who is your favorite character in the Star Wars saga?
Luke Skywalker. I think of it more of a universal thing. He embodies so much of everyone. Everyone starts out on a path; then circumstances change, and things happen, and you go to a new path. The thing that's always with him is the good. He's the good against the evil. He's looking out for Leia and Han Solo, too. So, he's got other people's best interests at heart. So the choices he makes are positively affecting not only him but the people around him. I think that's what so many people do in life, and that's probably why I feel like that. He's someone I can relate to.

What do you bring to Star Wars?
I'm still early on in my life, let alone in my career. But, hopefully, I'll bring freshness and self-confidence but with vulnerability. All the things that make me, that's what I'll bring to the character.

"SHE'S WORKED HARD IN COLLABORATION WITH J.J. TO MAKE REY LOVABLE AND SOFT, VULNERABLE, INNOCENT, BUT AT THE SAME TIME YOU BELIEVE THAT REY CAN BECOME STERN AND HARD AND KICK SOME BUTT, AND THAT'S WHAT SHE DOES." *–John Boyega, Finn*

"I started stunt training just a few weeks after I found out [I'd been cast]. We did hand-to-hand and used boxing to warm up. J.J. wanted me to look like I work out," Ridley says. "That was four hours a day, four days a week for three months. Without the guys we were training with, there's just no way John Boyega and I would have gotten through Abu Dhabi."

Ridley gets ready to race across the desert landscape aboard Rey's speeder. Opposite page: Rey comes face to face with Kylo Ren. "I'd love for people to leave the cinema thinking, aside from all the action and the fights, that it's an incredible story of people finding their place in a world," Ridley says.

Talk us through the training process. Your character is pretty badass.

I started stunt training just a few weeks after I found out. We did hand-to-hand and used boxing to warm up. J.J. wanted me to look like I work out. So I've been working the upper body. That was four hours a day, four days a week for three months. Without the guys we're training with, there's just no way John Boyega and I would have gotten through Abu Dhabi. The running stuff was so hard. It was a relief when there were explosions because we needed a break from the running. I haven't stunt trained for a while, but I'm still fitness training to keep the levels up. There are such long days that you need all the energy it brings.

What would you like to impart to young girls in this journey?

I would say be strong and be thoughtful and take care and realize how you're affecting other people. Learn and grow and don't be scared if things are offered to you that you're not sure about but may change your life. Dive in feet first. Take everything you can and appreciate every day. Appreciate the people around you who support you and never feel on your own because you never are.

A desperate escape from the clutches of the First Order leads to a violent crash as Finn's Special Forces TIE fighter meets a fiery end on the sands of Jakku. Concept artist Andrée Wallin's crashed starfighter design (inset) was precisely replicated in full scale on the blazing hot dunes outside Al Qasr, Dubai.

John Boyega as Finn

FINN STRUGGLES to escape his past. His previous name was just a serial number, FN-2187, and he was trained by the First Order to be a stormtrooper. Despite his great results in combat simulations, he was not prepared for a real, brutal battlefield. Sent to Jakku under the leadership of Captain Phasma, he couldn't follow orders and shoot innocent civilians. Dazed and scared, he chose to run away and stop being a cold-blooded soldier. FN-2187 doesn't believe he is a hero, but he can be one: He just needs to find something, or someone, worth fighting for.

Do you remember the moment when you were told you got the part?

I got an email from J.J. asking where I was. I told him I was at home, and he asked if I could get to a little café. I hopped in a cab, drove down and saw J.J. in the café by himself, drinking a cup of tea. We had a brief conversation, and he asked me whether I was ready, if this role could possibly happen. He asked me if I would be interested in working out and training, both as an actor and physically. He asked me if I realized how big the responsibility would be. I was like, "Yeah, I'll be fine. I'll do anything." Then he told me I was the new star in *Star Wars*. Everything stopped. I noticed everything. I noticed how many sugar cubes were in this little cup on the table. All the time it was going through my head: "He just said I'm the new star in *Star Wars*." I was willing myself to breathe.

Would you say that J.J. Abrams is celebrating the old in this new film?

I will say it's true that J.J. is definitely accepting the new with the CGI but also at the same time he is paying homage to the old with physical effects, and it has been amazing. I always think to myself, "What am I going to see with my very eyes today that's going to make me go, 'Wow, I'm filming *Star Wars*!'?" And there always is something.

Are you finding it fun to be surrounded by all the creatures?

I'm definitely having fun surrounded by the creatures. I am a big creature feature fan, and I love physical effects. I love the creatures being there right in my face. We have a great team that does the puppetry on these creatures. It's quite hilarious also because when the camera's not rolling they still stay in it, so the animatronics are still going, the puppetry's still going, so you find yourself having conversations with several different species you've never met before. It's a good time.

Do you have a favorite Star Wars film?

Return of the Jedi is my favorite film because you find Luke Skywalker at a very vulnerable time. In the first film he was learning who he is and learning about this special world that's out there that he never knew about. *Return of the Jedi* is a great mix of drama, comedy and somewhat expands the universe in terms of the Ewoks and other creatures that you find in the movie. It's my favorite because it's the establishment of each character at a different point in their lives.

"JOHN IS A FANTASTIC HUMAN BEING. I REALLY, REALLY HAVE A LOT OF AFFECTION FOR JOHN.… HE'S INCREDIBLY FLEXIBLE AND ON HIS TOES WITH DIFFERENT IDEAS. HE'S GOT A HUGE RESPONSIBILITY, AND I THINK THAT HE'S JUST DOING IT WITH A LOT OF GRACE AND GENEROSITY." *–Oscar Isaac, Poe*

It wasn't until halfway through the audition process that John Boyega learned Finn was one of *The Force Awakens*'s leads. "J.J. was like, 'You're the guy. You know that, right?'" remembers Boyega. "I was like, 'Ahh! OK, it's time to get acting chops together and do something!'"

"I was drenched in sweat by the time I got out of the stormtrooper outfit," Boyega says. So how did he endure the Abu Dhabi heat? "Let's just say it was a combination of sweat, passion, fandom, ice cubes, eye drops and a lot of water." Inset: J.J. Abrams oversees Boyega on set.

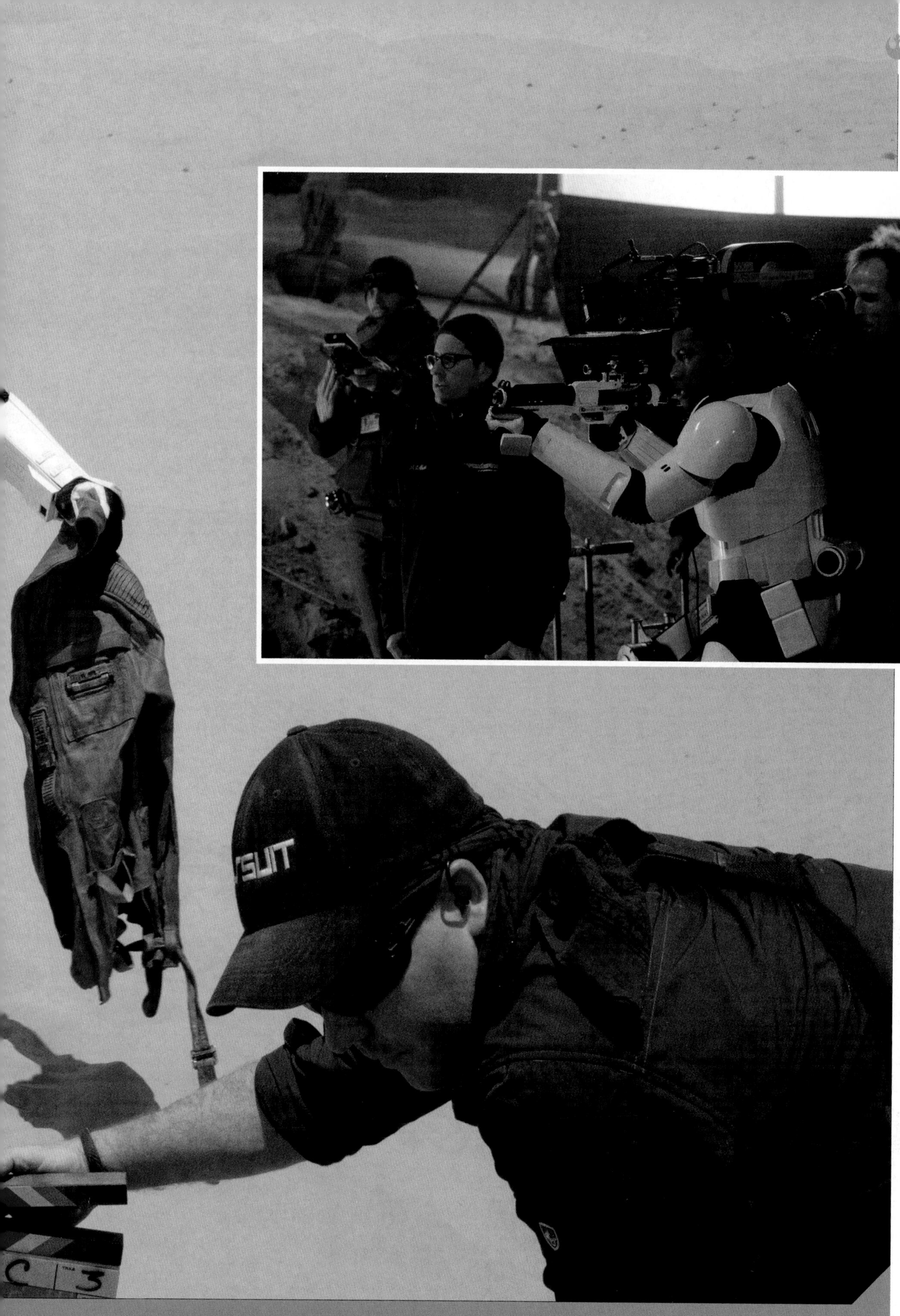

Oscar Isaac as Poe Dameron

OMMANDER POE DAMERON is the best pilot in the Resistance. This is why General Leia Organa sends him on a mission to retrieve a clue to Luke's location. Together with his loyal droid BB-8, Poe reaches Tuanul, a small, remote village on frontier planet Jakku. With the help of an old ally of the Resistance, the pilot completes his mission. But when the First Order stormtroopers attack the village, Poe has no other option but to entrust the secret information to BB-8 and send him away. While the battle rages, Poe looks for a way out alone.

How did you first get involved with The Force Awakens?

I got a call to come meet J.J. Abrams in Paris, and I showed up without any information as to exactly what it was. I had a vague feeling that it was about *Star Wars*, but even that was a bit under wraps. So I came to Paris and sat with him and Kathy Kennedy and Larry Kasdan, and they just told me about the film and the role that they were interested in me playing.

What was your reaction?

I just tried to stay cool and stay calm and listen and take it in. But really just utter excitement and a bit of disbelief that this was actually happening.

Were you a Star Wars fan?

I've been a *Star Wars* fan as an adult and a child. It was a big part of my family. My uncle, cousin and brother were huge *Star Wars* fans, and so they collected all the toys. So I, by proxy, was also a fan. The first film I remember seeing as a child was *Return of the Jedi*. I think for a lot of people in the film business in general, *Star Wars* is a milestone. For some people, it's why they do what they do, so to be asked to be a part of it was a huge, huge honor, and it just created such excitement.

How did J.J. Abrams give you his vision of the film?

J.J. Abrams spoke a bit about the vision of the film and also about how he wanted to approach the film by going back to the roots of it and shooting it on film, making it a very textured world. As far as the performances, it feels like he sees things on three levels, at least in the way that I see it. One is visually the story that's being told, so you can turn it on silent and still have communicated what's happening emotionally. Secondly, it's the energy, which is really the thrust of the whole thing. Then third is the nuance of the characters and how they interact with each other. Any suggestions I might have [character-wise] come from a place of how those three things get affected and how they can be highlighted. That was an interesting thing because with playing Poe, it's a specific color that he adds to the film. It's one that's energetic. There's almost an old-school *His Girl Friday* Cary Grant kind of quickness to it. That speed is something J.J. really likes.

Talk about the impressive scale of the film.

It's a real textured world and environment. You actually have two full-sized X-wings standing there that you can run up to and the cockpit will open. You can jump in and fire up. Apart from performance-wise, everyone that's

> "HE'S VERY ARTICULATE AND HAS A GREAT SENSE OF ART. HE DOES TAKE THIS VERY SERIOUSLY, AND ALSO AT THE SAME TIME WITH A CHARACTER LIKE POE, HE'S VERY CHARMING AND HANDSOME AND FUN." *–John Boyega, Finn*

Oscar Isaac as Poe Dameron, one of the best pilots in the galaxy. "My uncle is the biggest *Star Wars* fan," Isaac says. "When I told him I got cast in this, he was crying and could barely breathe."

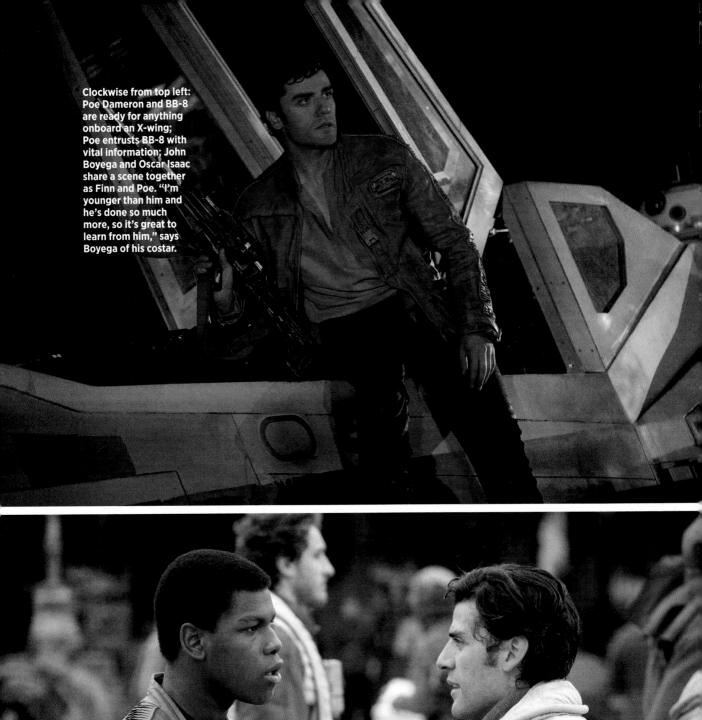

Clockwise from top left: Poe Dameron and BB-8 are ready for anything onboard an X-wing; Poe entrusts BB-8 with vital information; John Boyega and Oscar Isaac share a scene together as Finn and Poe. "I'm younger than him and he's done so much more, so it's great to learn from him," says Boyega of his costar.

involved feels like it's real and like it's there. It infuses the film with something that's unquantifiable. Being able to literally run through the sand and run up onto my X-wing, have the thing open and start up and everything light up, is unlike anything I've ever done before.

I've looked around all the sets, and they're done with such creativity. What I like about it, too, is that it's also a bit of a period piece because it goes back to the technology that they were using in the original films. There is a slightly '80s vibe that they're able to elicit with a lot of the designs and using actual everyday objects as well mixed into the set. That's just so great because, again, it's a reminder that it is part of a legacy and a culture. You're creating culture. That's something that Max von Sydow had said when we were sitting there talking a little bit. He said these movies create culture; they create a whole lineage and ancestry and world by all these little bits and pieces that they use. It infuses everything with meaning.

What will audiences take away from this?

What's great is that this is being done with no cynicism. It's being done open-hearted and with such love and such enthusiasm from everybody, starting with J.J. I think that's going to be infectious. You'll be able to feel that coming off the screen; just the love of *Star Wars* and the love of these stories and being able to add new ones to the legacy. J.J. has been doing it exactly how you would want these films to be handled. Obviously, they mean so much to everyone. Everyone has ownership over them. Everyone wants them to be their thing. That's always a difficult and scary thing because everyone has a very specific idea of what it should be. But I think when you approach it with this much love and generosity, that stuff becomes less important. You see that this is someone who loves it so much and has found people that love it just as much and who want to make it special and beautiful.

Flanked by First Order stormtroopers, Kylo Ren descends the ramp of his Command Shuttle to oversee an invasion force. Ryan Church created this piece primarily as a ship design, giving production a sense of what needed to be built and what could be digitally added later by Industrial Light & Magic.

Adam Driver as Kylo Ren

MPULSIVE AND ruthless, Kylo Ren is lost in darkness and hate. He once was a Jedi apprentice, but he betrayed his master Luke Skywalker, turning to the dark side of the Force. He joined the mysterious organization called the Knights of Ren, took a new name and became the apprentice of Master Snoke—the supreme and enigmatic leader of the First Order. Snoke trained Kylo Ren to use the power of the Force to inflict pain, invade the minds of his victims and kill them with no regret. Kylo considers himself immune to the light and is ready to prove it at any cost. He is also obsessed with Darth Vader and keeps the deformed mask of the fallen Sith Lord in his chamber, talking to it as if it were alive.

How much was J.J. Abrams able to share with you after you signed on?
J.J. Abrams pretty much walked me through the whole thing. He talked about how he wanted to start it and the themes that he was going with. He talked about things that inspired him that he and Larry Kasdan were already working on. There have been changing bits and pieces since then, but it's all pretty much the same. J.J. had very clear ideas in his mind about the conventions he wanted to upturn and things that grounded Kylo Ren as a character. Character was something that he talked about the most. I feel like some of the movies are so heavy on special effects or visuals and lot of things get lost as far as two people talking to one another. And that was something J.J. stressed from the beginning; it was all character, there was hardly any talk of special effects.

What sense did you have of taking on such a role?
The idea of doing it is a scary thing. Even though J.J. mapped out what that character does, he left out a lot of things for us to discover. He wanted to get my input, which was a huge thing also in a movie of this scale.

How cool and surreal is it to play this character?
Surreal is a good word to describe many things in this movie, but that's certainly one of them. Seeing everybody all in one room for the table read was surreal; I just wanted to sit back as an audience member and listen to them. I remember in the read-through that things would just come to life when the original characters read their parts. Suddenly I just wanted to sit back and watch and enjoy the movie, but then I realized I had lines to say and a part to play.

What makes Star Wars great?
At the end of it, I think the great thing about *Star Wars* is that, yes, it's a long time ago in a galaxy far away and there are spaceships and lightsabers, but the family story and the friendship and sacrifice elements are really big human themes that make it enduring. All those human things are what connected people to those movies in the first place.

Do you have a fun Star Wars memory?
I think everyone does. I feel like it was just part of childhood. Now, with the *Star Wars* movies being made or maybe because I'm more aware of it, all I think about is *Star Wars*. But in the sense of how much *Star Wars* has embedded itself into the culture. I always felt like it was part of my upbringing.

"THE MINUTE WE STARTED TO REALIZE THIS CHARACTER, IT JUST SEEMED OBVIOUS TO ME THAT ADAM WAS ONE OF THOSE RARE ACTORS THAT COULD EMBODY HIM. J.J. DIDN'T KNOW HIM AS WELL AS I DID, BUT THE MINUTE HE MET HIM HE INSTANTLY RESPONDED." **–Kathleen Kennedy, producer**

"It's interesting to find out who he is with the mask on or with the mask off," Driver says of the process of portraying Kylo Ren. "There's something empowering for someone to completely hide themselves in a mask that is so intimidating."

Han Solo and his loyal Wookiee first mate Chewbacca step foot on their freighter, the *Millennium Falcon*, for the first time in many years. Witnessing the emotional reactions of *The Force Awakens* cast and crew as they entered the perfectly recreated *Millennium Falcon* set was a favorite moment during the film's production. The visual concept for this scene was originally sketched out by artist Matt Allsopp (inset).

Harrison Ford as Han Solo

AN GAINED control of his destiny when he won his ship, the *Millennium Falcon*, playing sabacc—a popular card game. He has been a pirate and a smuggler, but after he met Luke and Leia he joined the Rebel Alliance and helped destroy the Death Star (twice!). Still, he prefers to introduce himself as a smuggler rather than a war hero.

When did you find out they were going to make new films, and what did J.J. tell you about his vision?

It was a couple years ago, but I didn't see a script until about a year and a half ago when I started getting involved. We had discussions about development of that character and his relationship to other characters in the story. They were very interesting and encouraging conversations. Then there was some work done in respect of the questions I had or input that I had with J.J. Abrams, and I was pleased with that. But I'm a "get on at the beginning" and "off at the end" kind of guy, so I don't really remember the street signs along the way.

What does J.J. Abrams bring to the table as a director?

He's very thoughtful and very wise about human nature and the development of character and relationships. He brings a real sincerity and emotional understanding to relationships, which is something I was very pleased to see. He's an enormously skilled filmmaker and very efficient director and producer. So it has been a real pleasure to work with him and all of the members of his team as this film has gone on.

Walking back on the Millennium Falcon set—what was that like?

I spent a lot of years here, so it was fun to see it again. I didn't remember it as well as I thought I did. There are things I remember about the cockpit and the funny stuff we went through. On the original cockpit, I asked George to let us get into it, so we could try it on for size. Finally, we did get a chance, Chewie and I, to walk into the cockpit. Of course, he couldn't get into the seat. Flying it developed a little bit between iterations of the first three films, but it started to come back to me. It was fun.

What is it like working with Daisy Ridley and John Boyega?

They are both very engaging personalities; both in their real lives and in their screen characters. I think the audiences will be delighted to make their acquaintance and follow them through the story. They're both very inventive and spirited presences. Their characters are very interesting and go through some interesting changes. The casting has been brilliant, in both cases.

What do you hope audiences will take away from this film?

Recognition of our common humanity and that all of us face the same kinds of problems in our lives, and that there's hope. There's joy in the celebration of right and wrong and in the recognition of truth that sustains us.

–On "Chewie, we're home."

"IT WAS AMAZING FOR EVERYBODY. I WAS SITTING BY THE MONITORS, NEAR THE DOOR OF THE *MILLENNIUM FALCON*, AND I TURNED AROUND AND THERE MUST HAVE BEEN 150 PEOPLE FROM THE CREW WHO HAD ALL QUIETLY GATHERED TO GET AROUND THE MONITORS AND SEE THAT MOMENT. IT WAS VERY EMOTIONAL. EVERYONE WAS FEELING SOMETHING SLIGHTLY HISTORIC WAS GOING ON. IT REALLY GAVE YOU CHILLS." *–Kathleen Kennedy, producer*

Harrison Ford reprises his role as Han Solo after more than 30 years. "I knew that the film would be in good hands, but that wasn't the only attraction to the project for me," Ford says.

Harrison Ford, Daisy Ridley and John Boyega on set for *The Force Awakens*. Of his seasoned costar, Boyega says: "As an artist, you're portraying a role, being an actor and performing. But the camera is the eye of the audience, so you have to also facilitate that. You have to facilitate the lighting, the positions and the visual effects. Harrison knows how to do all of that with great balance but also have fun and make it a comfortable set." Inset: Han Solo in a heated battle outside Maz's castle.

HAN'S GREATEST ONE-LINERS

"I don't know...fly casual!"

"Traveling through hyperspace ain't like dusting crops, boy."

"Never tell me the odds."

"We're all fine here now, thank you...how are you?"

"And I thought they smelled bad on the outside...."

"I know."

"Chewie, we're home."

Peter Mayhew as **Chewbacca**

WOOKIEE FROM the planet Kashyyyk, Chewbacca has long been loyal to Han Solo. Teaming with him, Chewbacca later became Han's best friend and copilot. Loyal and brave, he helped the Rebellion restore freedom to the galaxy. Chewie is 234 years old, but Wookiees are long-lived, so he is considered to be just in his prime.

Seeing Chewie just melts hearts. Why is that?

Chewie's a teddy bear. Everybody has had a teddy bear at some stage in their lives. He's lovable; he's cuddly. I don't know what it is. If I don't do anything else, this is my chance to go into the history books.

What was it like putting the suit back on?

Wonderful. It's a completely new suit. It's better. It's lighter. It looks as good as the original one, and it was built the same way. It was cut out, mask was made and all the fur was sewn into the yak hair stuff that they used for the costume. It works.

In the original films, how much was scripted for you and how much was you?

I'd say about 50/50. The way I looked at it, say we're in the cockpit. You've got four people in there. Chewie can't stand there looking like a piece of furniture. He has to react to everybody's attitude. And, he can't say verbally what he wants to, so, he either has to use his mouth, or eyes or body language of some sort. So, that was 50 to 70 percent. I expected to be fired the first week. But, fortunately, George Lucas saw what I was trying to do, and here we are many years down the road.

What did J.J. Abrams tell you about his vision?

It's going to look as original as possible. If you look around here, it is. I have pictures, black and whites, of stuff that was there of the old set. It's as good. In five years, if it were maintained, that's what this should look like. With the cockpit scenes, there are still only two levers that actually work. There were only two in the original, too.

What was it like coming to the **Millennium Falcon** set?

I knew it was going to be good, so I wasn't going to be too over enthusiastic. One person's idea of perfect is not everybody's. But, when I came up here and looked across and saw the bed over there. I was like, "Yeah, this is back." This is what it looked like when we did the shoot with Mark and Harrison and Carrie.

For the team to be together, was that a surreal moment?

It was wonderful. I hadn't seen Harrison in a good few years. It was so nice. Talk about a wonderful feeling. That kind of relationship lives on. It will always be Han and Chewie. It won't be anything but.

IMPOSING PRESENCE

"Will someone get this big walking carpet out of my way?"
–LEIA

"I suggest a new strategy, R2: Let the Wookie win."
–C-3PO

"Laugh it up, fuzzball."
–HAN SOLO

"I'd just as soon kiss a Wookiee."
"I could arrange that...you could use a good kiss!"
–LEIA AND HAN SOLO

As Chewbacca, Peter Mayhew takes the helm of the *Millennium Falcon*. Asked about auditioning for *A New Hope* in George Lucas's office, Mayhew said: "When George walked in, I stood up. The interview was just about over at that point."

Finn takes control of a lightsaber and his destiny during an attack outside Resistance base. "Our lightsabers are really heavy, so you do get a sense of this power and this force that's coming out of this weapon, and it does really do something to you. But you do have to be strong, and you do have to have skill," John Boyega says. "There was definitely a lot of John Williams coming from the speakers in the gym during training."

Carrie Fisher as Leia Organa

RINCESS LEIA Organa of Alderaan has been a key command figure in the Rebel Alliance and one of the greatest opponents of the Empire. Educated in martial and political arts, she was always on the front line and led the Rebels to victory. Strong-willed and resourceful, she couldn't let the dark side destroy what she fought for: while keeping her influence on the New Republic Senate, she becomes leader of the Resistance to stop the First Order before it's too late. In need of help, she looks for her brother, Luke, her only hope to triumph over evil.

When you met with J.J. Abrams to talk about his vision, what was your takeaway from that meeting?
What I felt like with J.J. Abrams is that he loved these films. It's not part of your history; it's part of your childhood. Little kids grew up watching this, and J.J. is one of those. And there's a tremendous responsibility to this thing that he treasured. He was taking that seriously. He was excited by it. There's responsibility that goes with that, and he seemed completely up for that.

Did you have any input into this film's Leia? Like the hair?
I wanted to use the iconic hairstyle that I had initially.

I wanted that hairstyle back. If nothing else, I wanted little old Leia to walk by a window wearing that hairdo on the way to the bathtub. Just show it once. But, no. I guess they thought it would be too distracting.

There's something about this film that will appeal to women. Don't you agree?
I think women have always felt that. A princess

Leia Organa weighs her options inside the Resistance base map room as those loyal to her cause look on.

"I ADORED HOW FEISTY CARRIE FISHER WAS. I COULD REALLY SENSE AND FEEL HER FIRE, AND IT WAS IMPORTANT TO ME AS A LITTLE GIRL TO SEE THAT KIND OF WOMAN. TO SEE HER RUNNING AROUND, BEING POWERFUL, BEING INVOLVED IN SO MUCH ACTION WAS DEFINITELY A BIG INFLUENCE." –*Gwendoline Christie, Captain Phasma*

Leia, Chewbacca and Han Solo reunite on the battlefield. Leia has always been a strong female lead, something she has in common with *The Force Awakens*'s Rey.

is someone who takes responsibility for their life and makes choices and has a life. She doesn't fall into things. Nothing has changed except the hair.

How was it meeting the new cast?
I was nervous and excited. We had a good time together. Everyone was nervous in different ways. Watching Daisy Ridley through the process of filming—she's grown enormously. She's very confident, very at ease. So, it's definitely a home to her.

John Boyega seems comfortable in his role.
John always seemed comfortable. John came into the situation very confident, ready to get at it.

How is Adam Driver doing as a villain?
Playing a villain, but you don't know you're a villain. This is your cause, and this is what Adam is doing. He's passionate, but he's also solitary.

Is it fun to see some of the original creatures?
It's like a *Star Wars* high school reunion.

How about having Anthony Daniels back as C-3PO?
That's awesome, and he looks exactly the same.

Do you think there is a part of Leia in you?
I am Princess Leia. Princess Leia is me. It's like a Mobius strip. My life has informed who she is, and

she's informed who I am and who I've had to be, based on experiences I've gone through and the courage that was required to go through some of that. So, a lot of her demeanor, her passion and her willingness to go on, I've found in me.

Tell us about the fans.
These people, this is their fairytale. This is what they grew up with, what their fantasies were propelled by. It was this other world. They belong to that other world, and they feel a part of that.

They feel like they know you and to an extent they do. The funniest thing to me, and the sweetest thing to me, is when they bring you a 3-week-old child wearing the Leia outfit. It's also seeing these tiny kids and the children know who you are. That's the oddest, sweetest, most fascinating aspect of it. These people were young when I was not necessarily. So it places you very much where you didn't quite realize you were.

What will they (the fans) take away from this?
I think they'll be happy to be in their home away from home again.

LEIA'S STYLE GUIDE

EPISODE IV	EPISODE V	EPISODE VI
A NEW HOPE	***THE EMPIRE STRIKES BACK***	***RETURN OF THE JEDI***
The single most famous hairdo in cinema history, Leia's signature buns are at once regal and intimidating.	In the field during the Battle of Hoth, Leia dons dual braids and abandons Episode IV's style parted down the middle.	While kept as a slave in Jabba's palace, Leia places her penchant for symmetry aside in favor of a long single braid.

Led by ace Resistance pilot Poe Dameron, a squadron of T-70 X-wing starfighters skim the surface of a lake on their way to battle in this concept art by James Clyne. Inspired by the film *Firefox*, *Star Wars: The Force Awakens* producer Bryan Burk pitched the idea of X-wings kicking up plumes of water as they speed along.

Domhnall Gleeson as General Hux

What was the table read like?

Carrie Fisher was there. Harrison Ford was there. Mark Hamill was there. Peter Mayhew was there. Everybody you'd hope to be there was there, plus all these new faces as well. I'd seen John Boyega in stuff. I'd seen Adam Driver in stuff and met him before. Andy Serkis, obviously. It was really exciting to look around at this amazing group of actors.

What will the movie bring to the universe?

How it feels to me is that J.J. Abrams is a very skilled director, and he's got this unusual combination of doing big movies in terms of scale and budget, but also working well with actors and telling real stories. All those things together are very unusual to get in the same person. A lot of people are good at one or two of those things. This is large-scale filmmaking that feels like a real story and isn't just effects. There's a real energy in the performances. They really get everyone going before a take, and you're reminded that this is *Star Wars* and that it requires a step up. So I hope the energy will be in the right place. I hope the story will move forward in a very interesting way. So, in the same way you'd watch one of the original three and not know what's coming next, I hope we can do that as well.

Have you visited the Creature Department and walked around Pinewood Studios?

I've walked around a little bit and seen some of the creature effects things, but also all the wardrobe department and the layouts and the setups for different costumes. I've seen a couple of the sets. I thought that with green screen coming in, I wasn't going to get to be on sets like this and that those days were over. They'd build in the three things you stand on and the rest would be green screen as far as you could see. That made me sad because when you're a kid and you think about what it must be like to be in movies, the scale of the ones you love was part of it. So, for me just walking around and seeing all this stuff and putting my hands on it, and it being tactile and present—I know how lucky I am to be on sets like this, and I'm enjoying it, that's for sure.

HUX IS a young and confident officer. He strongly believes all the systems in the galaxy will soon bow to the First Order and that the Resistance is powerless before the might of its army. Hux follows the orders of Supreme Leader Snoke, but he does not fear Kylo Ren or his powers.

How did you get the call to be in Star Wars?

I didn't have any meeting or any audition. But my big thing was I wanted to read the script before because they keep it tight. Then I got the call to meet J.J., so I flew over to meet him. I met with him and Lawrence Kasdan, which was a thrill in itself. J.J. told me about the character, what he was and what he did. They made an offer, and the next day was the table read with the cast. So, I stayed overnight, and the next day I was in the same room as these legends and new people who will go on to be legends themselves. So it was pretty cool and pretty fast. It all happened in two days.

"DOMHNALL REALLY CAPTURES THE VILLAINY AND REMINDS ME OF WHAT ALL THOSE GREAT ACTORS WERE CREATING WHEN THEY DID THE ORIGINAL TRILOGY. HE PLAYS THE PART PERFECTLY. EVERY SINGLE DAY HE WORKED, J.J. WOULD TALK ABOUT HOW AMAZING HE WAS." —*Bryan Burk, producer*

"General Hux is probably one of the bad guys, depending on your point of view," says Gleeson of his character. "He oversees the military organization and isn't a particularly nice fellow."

Gwendoline Christie as Captain Phasma

WEARING SPECIAL chrome armor, Captain Phasma commands legions of troopers with a firm hand—always remembering the serial number of each. She is constantly training, for she believes only the best soldiers can wear the armor of the First Order.

You are the first female stormtrooper of any rank. How does that feel?

I'm absolutely thrilled to hear that Captain Phasma is the first female stormtrooper, and of course I'm even more thrilled to be playing that part. It's exciting that something as iconic as *Star Wars* has embraced the future and has embraced the world's need for gender balance and female empowerment.

Talk us through your first scene.

I met J.J., properly, and we went through the scene. My heart was racing. I was so overexcited. But nothing prepared me for when I walked down out of the portal and turned into this studio and saw this entire set behind me, lit up and full of characters I recognized from years ago.

How is it to act in a helmet?

This glorious, majestic helmet—whose edges look as if they could cut you like a knife—seems as if it could cut through the night. It's futuristic but has a medieval element to it. When I put the helmet on, I feel like I could probably get away with blue murder. I'm going to wear it to walk home in tonight.

Tell us about Captain Phasma's weapon.

Captain Phasma has a phenomenal blaster. I've always wanted to work with a blaster. It's the most beautifully crafted thing. It does look real. It's quite weighty and very substantial. Everything on it works, although I haven't tried to blast anyone with it yet. It's just so beautifully designed. I have to be careful not to put my finger on the trigger because a light source will be released.

Can you talk about the powerful women in Star Wars and the fact that you're on the dark side of things?

I do think that in *Star Wars*, the iconic character of Princess Leia, for example, is a woman who has strength and the courage of her convictions, and isn't afraid to protect herself and to stand up for herself. Strong female characters interest me because they don't have to be brutal. They don't have to be physical. I'm incredibly lucky to be playing the part of a female character that is well rounded and that we see women, not just strong and good, but strong and evil, so we get to see all those recesses of human nature. They are all represented, and we can enjoy them. There is something faintly irresistible about Captain Phasma. I think it might be in the costume rather than me. Again, I think it's forward thinking and modern for *Star Wars* to have that kind of character archetype and to investigate that side of femininity. I'm incredibly privileged to be playing that part.

"WE WANTED TO GET SOME AMAZING WOMEN IN THIS MOVIE, AND THE EVILEST OF EVIL STORMTROOPERS WAS A PERFECT PART. GWENDOLINE CHRISTIE IS A GREAT CHOICE TO PLAY PHASMA." –*Bryan Burk, producer*

Gwendoline Christie looms large behind Captain Phasma's unique armor. Of her character, Christie says: "She is a malevolent force. She is not a force for good, and she takes particular pleasure in her cruelty."

The full might of the First Order is on display as General Hux gives an impassioned speech to his assembled forces. Massive military rallies throughout history, especially those of the Nazi Third Reich, provided the inspiration for this terrifying display of power and control, as envisioned by artist James Clyne (inset). Similar military assemblies appeared in earlier *Star Wars* films but none to this incredible scale.

Anthony Daniels as C-3PO

PROTOCOL DROID fluent in more than six million forms of communication, C-3PO faithfully served his masters, both Anakin and Luke Skywalker, never letting them down. With his counterpart, astromech droid R2-D2, he saw the end of the Republic and took part in the events that led to the end of the Empire. C-3PO now serves Leia Organa and the Resistance and is in contact with many droids who serve their masters in every corner of the galaxy: Together they form a network, which can be alerted in times of need.

Tell us about your history as C-3PO.

It's odd for me to realize 40 years of my life have been spent playing C-3PO. He's changed over the various generations of films because I have been in all seven movies now. I'm the only person to be involved in all of those movies, which is really strange. One of the reasons that is possible is because C-3PO isn't human. He's very human inside: He gets old inside and he gets more tired and cranky inside, but on the outside he's just who you first met back in 1977. For a lot of people, that's a very strong connection. It's helped me be a part of this extraordinary saga.

Many people will know, who are into the saga, that way back in 1975 when my agent said there's this American named George Lucas making this sci-fi movie, and he wants to see you for the part of a robot, I said no, since I wasn't interested in sci-fi, and she was amazed that a young actor could turn down an interview for any job. She was strong enough to say, don't be so stupid. So I did go and meet George, and he was very nice. But the thing that changed my mind, absolutely, was Ralph McQuarrie's original concept painting of C-3PO, set in another world, a strange moonlit planet. For some reason, that is what captured my imagination. This face just stared out of the picture. He had a companion, a strange sort of Swiss Army knife kit next to him, who knew what that was going to be? I had no idea what was going on at the time. In that moment, seriously, the eyes of the character penetrated my soul.

You are the only actor to appear in all the films. Can you elaborate on that?

Star Wars is a lot about destiny. Because of the character that I was given to play and because of George's concept of continuing storytelling, C-3PO was a rope on a life raft that you could cling to in all the films; the idea that if C-3PO is here, it must be a *Star Wars* film. For me, it's a real time trip. But, amazingly, my destiny is to be picked for a character that can time travel. And, of course, we're back.

How was it to be in character with Harrison Ford and Carrie Fisher again? Is it a pinch yourself moment?

I was thinking the other day, that way back in 1977 I'd take Mark, Carrie and Harrison to the local Indian restaurant in London. The other night, there we were bowling, in a bowling alley, with Carrie. Tonight I'm off with Mark and his family to a fish and chip shop in London where we live. That's the normalcy: You can do wacky stuff in the day then do fish and chips. Being in scenes with these characters just feels right. Doing a scene with Carrie the other day, particularly when we're in rehearsal, I can just look straight into her eyes, her beautiful eyes, and she can look straight back to my bloodshot ones, and we have total understanding of what we're talking about.

Do you have the same costume as before? Have there been any tweaks?

In *The Force Awakens*, C-3PO is pretty much back to how you would remember him. There are tiny nuances that are different. Some of them are technical on the inside, and that's for me to know. But there are other little additions, and fans will enjoy that. The big one, which is a deep, deep secretive element I'm going to share with you. In the first film, *A New Hope*, C-3PO's left leg was silver and nobody ever noticed

C-3PO keeps a watchful eye on R2-D2 at Resistance base. "Ben Burtt's sounds made such a difference," says Anthony Daniels on his surprisingly human costar. "Suddenly I was seeing a two-way conversation, and it was magical."

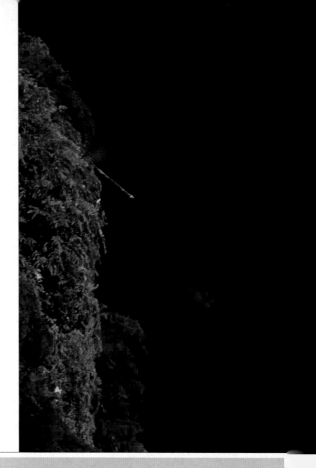

because it was light silver, which would merely reflect the gold or the desert or the sand. George Lucas's original idea was that C-3PO had a history. The idea that *Star Wars* didn't just happen out of nowhere; it wasn't page one of a story. It was page one million of an age-old story of good and evil. One of George's concepts is that characters should be broken down, used, scratched. This makes you think something has happened in the past. He has a history.

Move forward, and J.J. Abrams takes that idea several notches higher. C-3PO—I don't know how he feels about it, but I don't think he's happy about it because he is a purist—has a red arm. His left arm is a fairly brutal, red, rusty, sanguine thing. Something has happened to him in the last 30 years. The Rebels have had all sorts of dramas, and one of his was clearly losing a limb. In Episode VIII or by Episode IX, it would be nice to be back in one piece.

BB-8: OUR ONLY HOPE

THE NEWEST ADDITION TO THE RICH STAR WARS TRADITION OF MECHANICAL CHARACTERS HAS A FAMILIAR TASK: DELIVERING SECRETS TO THE REBELS.

BB-8 is more than just a spherical astromech droid. It's a trusty Resistance agent and the loyal and enthusiastic helper of pilot Poe Dameron. BB-8 would face any danger to stay close to its companion. Agile and particularly fast, this little droid always tries to go unnoticed, as its self-preservation protocols require.

BB-8 controls its body—made of six circular tool-bay discs—through wireless telemetry. An internal orbiculate motivator rolls it, while magnetic casters keep its head still. BB-8's language is a new-generation variant of the common astromech language.

THE CAST WEIGHS IN

BB-8 is amazing. BB-8 is so cute and charismatic...and a little bit feisty. I'm starting to wonder if

R2-D2 is a distant cousin. BB-8 is lovely to work with. I have to talk about BB-8 as an actor because BB-8 is actually there on set. On *Star Wars* we're not messing around. It's puppetry; it's animatronics, and BB-8 is a combination of both. It's been amazing working with BB-8. But sometimes he's a bit rude and has to work on his attitude.
—JOHN BOYEGA

BB-8 is going to be loved by everyone. He's so small—so much smaller than R2-D2—and because he's puppeteered, he's alive. He was the first character I had a real scene with, and I was nervous because he's not a human being. But, because of the puppeteers, he comes alive. BB-8 is brilliant. He's amazing.
—DAISY RIDLEY

His design is amazing. I believe J.J. Abrams actually came up with the design, which is so ingenious because it feels like I've seen it before. It feels like it's familiar to the *Star Wars* universe, but it's not; it's completely new. The fact that it's a ball that moves around, it looks like he has a little belly; it's very cute, but he's so expressive because of that and has so much more room for expression. He really comes to life, and they have so many different versions of him. They have a puppeteer who's in a blue suit or green suit, there's one by himself that's remote controlled, and there's a stationary one.
—OSCAR ISAAC

Creating the Creatures

SIMON PEGG, FULL-BLOWN
STAR WARS FANBOY AND THE
ACTOR WHO BRINGS UNKAR PLUTT
TO LIFE IN *THE FORCE AWAKENS*,
ON HOW PRACTICAL EFFECTS
MAKE THE FILM FEEL REAL.

ow cool is it to be in Star Wars?
There's not a register that it can possibly be measured on. For me it's the culmination of everything that made me want to be an actor and be part of this world. It's my childhood dream realized. This is me within the environment that made me want to be a film actor. It doesn't get any cooler than that. To be able to hug Chewie and lean on R2-D2, talk to Carrie Fisher and Mark Hamill—these are the things that I dreamt of as a kid.

As a fan, were you impressed with the creatures for The Force Awakens?
Yes. Amazing stuff. I love the fact that they got in some of the guys from *War Horse* to do some of the puppeteering. There's a lovely story, actually, that I told J.J. A long time ago, I was watching *The Empire Strikes Back* with my daughter, who was 3 at the time. When we were watching the movie and Frank Oz's Yoda puppet came on the screen for the first time, my daughter, who had only ever seen Yoda as a photograph, turned to me and said, "Oh, daddy, he's real." I was so blown away by that. It was a very honest reaction, and I just gave her a big hug because I was so proud that she saw he was there, and that, yes, he was a puppet but he was real. I told this to J.J., and J.J. took that story into a number of meetings when he was sort

of establishing how this film was going to be made.

Physical must never be let go of. CG is a wonderful tool, but it has its place; it shouldn't do everything. Once it starts doing everything, the film will become a cartoon. Whereas if you use real stuff that actors can interact with and be there with, there's a feeling of proximity and jeopardy that you cannot achieve with CG entirely. So it's wonderful to see all this stuff being made.

1. Grummgar, a new entry into the pantheon of imposing *Star Wars* creatures. 2. Senior Sculptor Luke Fisher brings one of *The Force Awakens*'s creature concepts into reality.

2

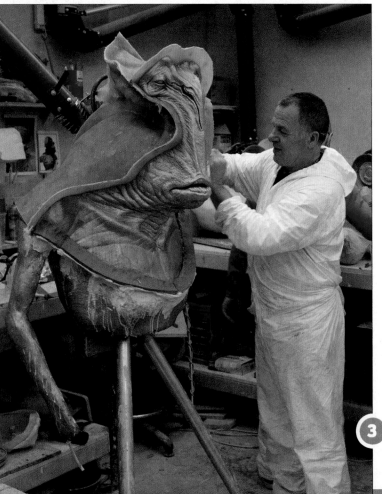

What is your costume like?

We did all the close-up work at Pinewood because the mask had to be glued to my face so the articulation was there. We couldn't do that in Abu Dhabi because of the heat, so we used the pull-over mask, which is nevertheless still as much rubber. Then there's sort of a fat suit and rubber gloves. It was extremely hot and worryingly, at times, claustrophobic. My heart rate would go up a little bit, and I just haD to keep going, "It's *Star Wars*. It's *Star Wars*."

But this is what you do in *Star Wars*. You get into ridiculous outfits and makeups, and you suffer because it's so much better if it's real, if you're there, and if it's a genuine thing that is interacting with actors, not just a digital creation. So I was prepared to suffer without complaint as I melted, literally, inside this silicone prison.

Did you do a whole-body cast?

I did. I had an upper body cast, actually, which meant they cast my head, my shoulders and my neck for the prosthetic. And then they cast my torso for me to fit into the suit. It's an interesting process.

Tell us about Neal Scanlan and his crew?

Neal is extraordinary. I remember when we were out in Abu Dhabi and they built this little thing that comes out of the sand and looks like a classic *Star Wars* creature. It's on a sort of hydraulic and then it goes back down, and I just remember thinking, these guys are having a blast on this. I would probably bet that the vast majority of guys and girls working on this in physical effects were inspired by *Star Wars*.

What elements make this a Star Wars film?

I think when you watch the movie, it will feel very much like *Star Wars*. You will see that in the physical effects element, the practical sets, the makeups and the masks. All these things are present, and that makes a huge difference. When you see computer-generated stuff, if it's obviously computer generated, it stops you from thinking about how they did it because you have an abstract idea of how they do that. Someone does this in a room and then that appears. That is somehow less awe inspiring and less impressive than seeing a real, full-size *Millennium Falcon* sitting in a forest. I think that's what J.J. completely gets in terms of what makes *Star Wars* amazing.

1. Kiran Shah (performer), Waldo Mason (Sculptor and Skin Development), James Sandys (Senior Animatronic Designer), Neal Scanlan (CFX and SMUFX Creative Supervisor) and Paul Bodycote (Creature Choreographer) help get one of Jakku's finest up and running. 2. Some of the rough and tumble denizens of Maz's castle, including Warwick Davis as Wollivan. 3. Senior Mold Maker Terry Sibley hard at work in the creature effects department. 4. Modeler Justin Pikethly helps give a creature a hand. 5. Worrts gets a final look before filming.

Do you think the film honors skill sets that we don't see much anymore?

I think so. I think it harkens back to a time when necessity was the mother of invention. You had to think on your feet. It's so easy to fix things in the computer these days; so easy to let it be done in post or brush it aside and let someone do it. That's not to downplay the skill of CG because it's an extraordinary tool. I always compare it to synthesizers. Back in the 1980s when the synths first appeared, everybody thought there would be no more drums, no more guitars—that it was all going to be synths. There was a period where everybody was using them and everybody overused them, and then eventually they became part of the pantheon of music making, and they found their place. I feel like CG is like that. CG had a big period of like, "we can do anything," and then realizing that yes, you can, but it's not necessarily wholly constructive to do everything that way. Now CG has become a valuable, extraordinary tool in a vast array of tools we have in the film industry. That's what this film will demonstrate because, yes, we'll have incredible physical effects and stuff that is happening in camera, and there will be digital stuff that is extremely amazing and brilliantly done and skillfully rendered. It's a question of how you use things. J.J.'s got the mix just right on this.

1. The gambling tables at Maz's castle are at once original and reminiscent of *Star Wars* locations such as the Mos Eisley Cantina.
2. Creature Choreographer Paul Bodycote on location with one of his "actors," a happabore, in Abu Dhabi.

Anything can (and does) happen inside Maz's castle. "We have a great team that does the puppetry on these creatures," John Boyega says. "It's quite hilarious also because when the camera's not rolling they still stay in it, so the animatronics are still going, the puppetry's still going, so you find yourself having conversations with several different species you've never met before. It's a good time."

The Saga Continues

DIRECTOR J.J. ABRAMS ON HIS LOVE OF THE *STAR WARS* FRANCHISE, AS WELL AS HIS AFFECTION FOR THE ACTORS WHO ARE HELPING TO CARRY IT FORWARD.

What does Star Wars *mean to you?*

It's funny, but I remember the first time I saw the words "*Star Wars*." It was in a *Starlog* magazine, a very geeky sci-fi magazine. I remember seeing the words, and saying them aloud, "*Star Wars*." There was something about it that felt unusual, and that was before the film came out. But, it stuck with me. I was 11 years old, and seeing the film for the first time—it was mind expanding. It was full of heart and romanticism and optimism and comedy and incredible conflict, and certainly visual effects like I had never seen before. It was such a profound thing. Not just because the movie itself was so entertaining, but because it said anything is possible. It said not only you could be anything you want to be, but there was a righteous fight to join. There were friends in the world and allies you'd come across; there was majesty that could come out of simplicity and intimate relationships. It was such a great story of the underdog and told with such great imagination. When you look at *Star Wars*, it is unbelievable how much they got right. Not just the story and the characters and the casting. Not just the design, not just the music. All of it. When you look at all of it, you realize how much was nailed...even the references to things that happened off camera. The things you don't know. You don't know so much in that movie, like what the Empire wants or the possibility that Vader is Luke's father or Leia's his sister. All these things exist, but none are explicit. Yet, it has that sense that this world is real and exists and is expansive. It felt beautifully considered and wonderfully told. For me, as a kid, it bowled me over. It's a world I wanted to get back to immediately, and I was in good company.

Talk about Daisy Ridley. What was it about her?

We looked for a long time at many people. What we were looking for was someone who felt that she was capable of everything. It's a crazy thing, but this character needed to be brought to life by an actor that didn't have limitations. We needed someone who was going to be vulnerable, tough, terrified, thoughtful, sweet and confused to take on the burden of this role and do it with authenticity. We needed someone who is able to go to this deeply emotional state and do it again and again, in some cases with brand-new actors; in other cases with actors that didn't exist at all and in other cases, legendary actors. She needed to do all of this, and on top of everything, be an unknown.

I didn't want someone who everyone knew who you had seen before in that other thing. To find someone no one knew, who could do all these things, took a lot of looking. Luckily we had Nina Gold, Theo Park and April Webster in the States working to help us find this person. It was a long search, as it needed to be. We found some great people, but it wasn't until we found Daisy that we thought we'd found the person who can do that sweet, light stuff; she has an incredible smile. She's beautiful. She could do the spirited stuff as well as the tough and emotional.

When she started doing fight training, she had such ferocity. She does this ferocious, gritting of her teeth, primal strength thing that she can do. On the

"J.J. WAS CERTAINLY ONE OF MY FIRST CHOICES. I THINK *STAR WARS* HAS THIS UNIQUE SENSIBILITY; THIS COMBINATION OF ADVENTURE AND FANTASY AND HUMOR. THERE ARE VERY FEW DIRECTORS WHO EMBODY ALL OF THOSE SENSIBILITIES AS AN ARTIST. J.J. IS ONE OF THE FEW." *–Kathleen Kennedy, producer*

J.J. Abrams and producer Kathleen Kennedy on location outside Resistance base. "J.J. and I said right away that when we cast this movie, we would make it more diverse than the way you perceive *Star Wars* was made in the 1970s," Kennedy says. "We wanted to make it more reflective of society today."

J.J. Abrams gives BB-8, or at least its puppeteers, a little direction in Abu Dhabi. Inset: Abrams and Daisy Ridley discuss Rey's next move. Ridley is standing on the leg of a fallen AT-AT, a not-uncommon site on Rey's home planet following the Battle of Jakku.

one hand she's very relatable and delicate and new and innocent, and at the same time she's insanely wise. And wildly tough. She's sort of limitless in what she can do. So, when she came in, it was clear we had someone who was going to be enormously special and make a big impact. We realized it had better be in this movie. She's too good to pass up.

Tell us about John Boyega as Finn.

John's name came up very early on. It was a pitch that Larry had when we were talking about the backstory of these characters. This idea that there was a guy underneath the uniform that became a main character in the film, and one of our central heroes, was really interesting. The only time we had seen people in stormtrooper uniforms was when Luke and Han put them on to help save Leia. It felt like a great beginning of something. Whether he was a spy, or a turncoat, we knew it was an exciting way into this world. It felt immediately like we hadn't seen it before. The other thing thematically that I loved was it spoke to "who are you behind that mask?" The other thing a main character as a stormtrooper did was it thematically connected to this idea of who are these people behind these masks? All the new characters when we meet them are masked. Kylo-Ren is masked; Rey is masked when you first meet her, and Finn.

Where did Kylo Ren come from?

We needed a villain in the shadow of Darth Vader, one of the greatest movie villains ever. How do you create a bad guy that works in his shadow? Part of the beauty of the answer was in the character acknowledging himself that he was in the shadow of this character. He was as aware of Vader as we are. We wanted to give his villainy a conflict and not make him necessarily the mustache-twirling, finished villain but rather make him someone who is broken. A villain who's in process; a villain in training. We wanted to make him someone who is aspiring to certain greatness on the dark side. That was as much as a critical discussion between the two of us as anything.

Chewbacca, Han Solo and Finn outside the imposing walls of Starkiller base. On working with Harrison Ford, John Boyega says: "He hangs out with us after filming. I took him to southeast London to a nice Nigerian restaurant. He spoke to me about all the things that he'd been through and all the things he'd seen over the years as an actor. It was great to learn from him."

From Page to Screen

LAWRENCE KASDAN, WHO PENNED SCREENPLAYS FOR *THE EMPIRE STRIKES BACK* AND *RETURN OF THE JEDI*, ON RETURNING TO THE STAR WARS UNIVERSE.

You have a long history with* Star Wars. *Tell us about it.
I met George Lucas in 1977. I had sold a screenplay to Steven Spielberg. Steven and George decided, based on that screenplay, that they wanted me to write *Raiders of the Lost Ark*. I was thrilled to do that. I was brand new in the business, and it was an amazing job to get for your first job. When I was finished with it, I took it up to Marin County to deliver by hand to George Lucas. He threw it on the desk and said, "C'mon, let's go to lunch." When we went to lunch, he said he was in trouble with *The Empire Strikes Back* because Lee Bracket, who was working on it, had passed away, and there was no draft that was anything like what George needed or wanted.

He asked me to write *The Empire Strikes Back*. I was concerned because he hadn't read *Raiders of the Lost Ark*, but he said he would read it that evening and if he didn't like it, he would retract the offer. He did read it, and I began working on *The Empire Strikes Back* several days later.

When did you first meet J.J. Abrams?
I had met J.J. in 1999 at a charity event in Hollywood. He was very friendly, and I was happy to meet him. I had a wonderful, positive impression of him. After I became involved in the new saga, the question came up on who was going to direct Episode VII. Kathy Kennedy was very generous in including me in that process. When we went to talk to J.J., who was every-body's first choice, I started to get to know J.J. for the first time. That was in early 2013. We all went to his office and talked about what a new *Star Wars* would be like. His ideas about what should happen in the next trilogy were like mine, and I was enthusiastic about the idea that he'd direct it.

Did you and J.J. Abrams feel that the lead was always going to be a strong female?
There was never a question. It was not just J.J. and I but Kathy and everyone involved as well. We aimed very strongly toward one of the protagonists being a woman right from the get-go. It cries out for that. Leia was a wonderful character, but she was among the only women in the movie. This saga demands more in female leadership. We want to see more characters like that.

With the original cast returning, how much fun was it to revisit those characters?
It's great to come back to characters you love. Leia and Han are great people to write for, and now I've done it a lot. For someone who is their age, there's poignancy about how we lose our physical resilience. We deal with many things over a course of a lifetime. Some take a toll, and some show up in lines in our face. When you stop resisting it, it can be a glorious thing. You can appreciate, and you're grateful for this journey that put you through so many different paces. When you see Carrie Fisher and you see Harrison Ford, you see all that. We've followed them since they were so young. They grew up on camera.

"Chewie, we're home" is a cinematic moment. How did you come up with scenes like that?
We were very pleased when we wrote that scene. There were so many moments in writing, and it took months and months of J.J. and I alone walking, talking, sitting, writing. But we did it with a lot of walking around cities: Los Angeles, New York, Paris and London. I've never written a movie that way. We were talking and recording, and then we'd go someplace and write it down. It was so much more fun than normal writing. We were sitting at a café in Paris, one of the famous cafés where Hemingway sat, writing *Star Wars*, with J.J.'s computer on the table. We wrote a lot of it walking around Santa Monica, ending up at the Palisades looking at the Pacific Ocean on a gorgeous day. Once it was freezing cold, walking around Central Park. We were doing all the difficult work of story construction in incredibly pleasant circumstances. It was heavenly.

Director J.J. Abrams and Lawrence Kasdan share a moment together on a Star Destroyer interior set. "I have to hand it to Michael Arndt, J.J. Abrams and Larry Kasdan," says producer Kathleen Kennedy. "I think they found a very exciting story that honors all those things that George Lucas so meticulously created."

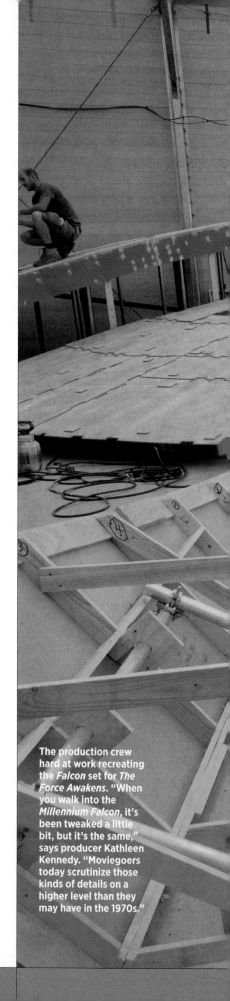

"You've Never Heard of the Millennium Falcon?"

IT MADE THE KESSEL RUN IN LESS THAN 12 PARSECS, AND IT'S JUST AS MEMORABLE IN *THE FORCE AWAKENS*.

T MAY SEEM like a hunk of garbage, but it's one of the fastest ships in the galaxy. This remarkable Corellian pirate vessel began its life as a YT-1300 light freighter, but went through significant remodeling. Its engines have doubled in size, its defenses are military-grade destructive weapons and its velocity and maneuverability are extraordinary. It's also an icon in the *Star Wars* saga.

"The *Millennium Falcon* is as much a returning character in the film as the people," says director J.J. Abrams. "There's a very weird feeling going back to something you know so well. It's like saying, 'I'm going to open this magic door.' And, behind this magic door is your bedroom at 9 years old. You can walk into that bedroom, and you can feel it, and smell it, and open drawers in your desk and find the things you had. What would be in that desk? What would be under your bed? That feeling of it's yours, and you know it. So, when you go back to it, it has to look like what you remember. It has to be what you know."

In order to create something that felt like the original from scratch, Abrams and his team were both meticulous and relentless, ensuring the sets they were building didn't just evoke the *Falcon* of the previous *Star Wars* films: They were the real thing.

"We made sure we almost forensically recreated the *Falcon*," Abrams

The production crew hard at work recreating the *Falcon* set for *The Force Awakens*. "When you walk into the *Millennium Falcon*, it's been tweaked a little bit, but it's the same," says producer Kathleen Kennedy. "Moviegoers today scrutinize those kinds of details on a higher level than they may have in the 1970s."

A BRIEF HISTORY

PLENTY HAS HAPPENED TO THE WORKHORSE OF A SHIP SINCE THE SECOND DEATH STAR.

Smuggler **Lando Calrissian** comes to own the *Falcon* through gambling.

Han Solo wins the ship from Lando in a heated card game.

Someone called **Ducain** steals the *Falcon* from Han Solo.

A gang called the **Irving Boys** steal the *Falcon* from Ducain.

Junk dealer **Unkar Plutt** steals the *Falcon* from the Irving Boys.

Rey, **Finn** and **BB-8** steal the *Falcon* from Unkar Plutt.

Han Solo and **Chewbacca** get the *Falcon* back.

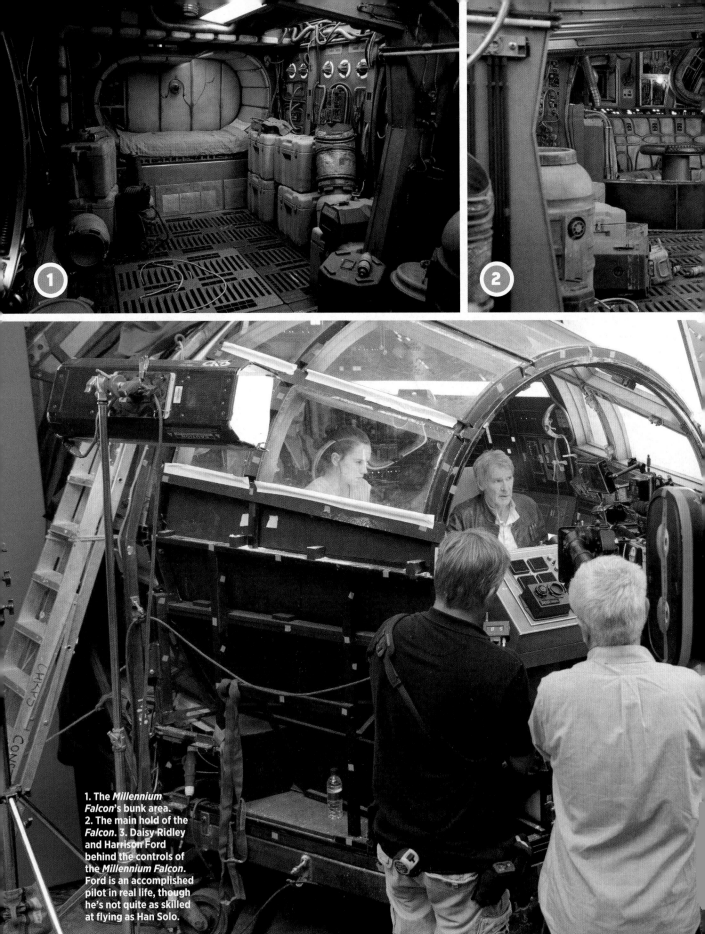

1. The *Millennium Falcon*'s bunk area.
2. The main hold of the *Falcon*. 3. Daisy Ridley and Harrison Ford behind the controls of the *Millennium Falcon*. Ford is an accomplished pilot in real life, though he's not quite as skilled at flying as Han Solo.

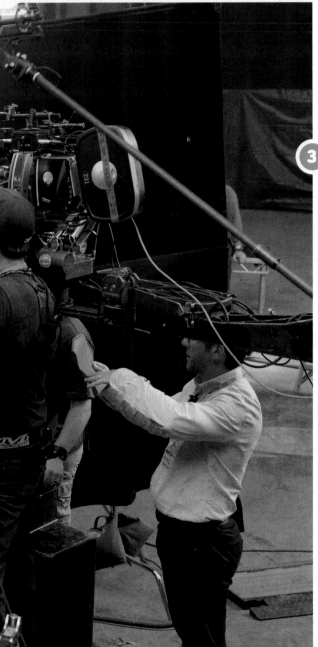

says. "I can't say enough about the crew. Our art director, Mark Harris, who worked on *The Empire Strikes Back*, was like a scientist figuring out how the *Falcon* changed from *Star Wars* to *Empire*." Among the adjustments Harris noted were an increase in the size of the cockpit, as well as the ship itself. This revelation allowed the filmmakers to feel comfortable making a few tweaks of their own—not unlike Han and Chewie over the course of the *Star Wars* saga. "We realized that with the stuff you thought was canon, big changes were being made," Abrams says. "You can't adhere to what you think it was, and do what they did. If something needs adjusting, go for it." There is, of course, a limit. "Aesthetically, it can't look or sound different than the ship you know," Abrams says. "An incredible amount of human hours were put into it and making it as we know it."

The actors were certainly convinced. "It's such an iconic set, and J.J. really wanted it to be perfect, so there was no mistaking what we're trying to create," Daisy Ridley says. "It's just so big. There are moments where I'm like, 'I'm flying the *Millennium Falcon*!'"

MODIFICATIONS

THE *FALCON* HAS BEEN USED FOR A LOT MORE THAN THE CARGO MISSIONS IT WAS BUILT FOR, AND IT HAS THE SPECS TO PROVE IT.

- The *Falcon*'s customized hyperdrive system is twice the size of the one in a standard YT-1300 freighter, making it twice as fast as any other warship.

- The *Falcon* sports military-grade armor, quad-laser cannons and many other illegal and customized hot-rod components.

- Over the years, laser hits and micrometeoroid punctures have been patched with micro-panels, giving the ship a dilapidated appearance.

- Unkar Plutt installed a special fuel pump that makes the *Falcon* even faster. But it must be primed in order to use hyperspeed.

- The old sensor rectenna, the large dish-shaped sensor and communication array, has been replaced after the original was sheared off during the attack on Death Star II.

1. The open-air market on Jakku. The Jakku market's interior, where parts and supplies of varying values are sold, swapped or stolen.

Setting the Scenes

●●●●

BRYAN BURK, ONE OF THE PRODUCERS OF *THE FORCE AWAKENS*, TALKS ABOUT CREATING THE WORLDS AND WONDER OF THE *STAR WARS* UNIVERSE.

ow difficult was it to create a sequel that so many people have been anticipating for so long?
The process of putting together the *Star Wars* film for us was a very natural and easy process. Particularly in the beginning, because as fans of the *Star Wars* Universe we just started talking about all the things that we love. All of us involved were able to articulate what we remembered from our childhood and what we loved when we went to the theater for

the first time and what we experienced. If we were to see another *Star Wars* film, what is it that we'd want to experience again? The whole process was just discussing things that we love in *Star Wars* and would want to see in the *Star Wars* sequels if we weren't working on them.

Summarize what is so special about Star Wars.
Star Wars really represents my youth and my childhood, and I could really remember that visceral experience of going to see the film at the AVCO

Theater in Westwood Village in Los Angeles when I was growing up. I'd never seen anything like it; it was tangible, and I could take it home with me. I remember, literally, the first LP I ever got was the soundtrack to *Star Wars*, and just sitting in my room and looking at the double-fold album cover and listening to John Williams's music and being catapulted back into the cinema. This is before there were VHS and videotapes or DVDs or obviously Internet. So, you couldn't relive it unless you were in the theater, but by just listening to that music and looking at Darth Vader's mask, I was there; I was back. It was something that you just had to experience over and over and over.

Walking onto these stages and seeing X-wings and seeing the *Millennium Falcon* and having the opportunity to walk up the ramp and onto the *Falcon* is like the adult version of being able to walk into Willy Wonka's chocolate factory.

Why did you choose to use practical sets and creatures?

When we started talking about working on the new film, we started thinking about all the things we loved in the original *Star Wars* films. It's amazing and hard to even visualize that at the time they were made there were no computer visual effects, and everything was tangible and they actually had to make things. There was this real artistry that has translated into all the artists who are working now on visual effects and computer animation. But a lot of the tactile puppetry that went into it or model-making or matte paintings, those artists have not been embraced in the same way, particularly in present-day films. So we wanted to go back to it and find all those artists who used to work on films like that, and in some cases, their parents who had

worked on them doing the same kinds of crafts and skills. We really wanted to make this film tangible and real. Even though you can create anything now with visual effects, the idea that it's even 1 percent slightly more real because it's tangibly there, and you can touch it and it's sitting there, makes all the difference in the world.

Where do you even start? What were the early processes?

We started with research. Research was an interesting process for this film. First of all, because it's *Star Wars*, there are numerous people out in the world who are die-hard fans, and they happen to be a lot of our friends. So we can have conversations with them, and they knew about the lore and what was missing or what had been heard to be lost in the archives or whatever it may be. So, to have the opportunity to go up to George Lucas's ranch and to go to the archives to see all this amazing artwork done by all of these amazing artists was incredible.

So much of Ralph McQuarrie's work was never used, so we put it in this film. Why not? It's gorgeous and totally timeless. On top of it, meeting people like Pablo Hidalgo at Lucasfilm who are beyond experts on the world of *Star Wars*—and know everything about it from the expanded universe to all the films— was an invaluable aid in making this film. A lot of the department heads existed before we even got involved. Rick Carter, the production designer, who is a genius, worked with Kathy Kennedy for years on numerous movies before. He was like no production designer I'd ever worked with in the sense that for him it wasn't just about the look of the movie, it was about the feel of the movie and the tone of the movie. We really just started talking about story with

1. The ground level of Maz's castle, a new hive of scum and villainy. 2. The corridor of a Star Destroyer. 3. The map room of Resistance base, a stronghold of hope in the galaxy.

Rick, who was involved in all the story meetings throughout the entire process. He understood the franchise and the film itself—what we wanted it to be and what Kathy wanted it to be.

What kind of experience is this for you as a producer?

Every time you make a movie or a television show, it's always a challenge, and you always hope you don't mess it up and hopefully people like it. In this case, it is no different and no more difficult than anything we've worked on despite it being a bigger title. But in this case, on this one occasion because we are such die-hard fans and love this movie so much, our approach has been: Let's make a *Star Wars* film that we would want to see if we were not working on the film. So, I believe that everyone involved is really excited about it and really believes in it because what we are doing is the kind of film, the kind of content, the types of characters and the return to the *Star Wars* Universe that we all love so much. Hopefully, once it's out in theaters, people will embrace it the way we all have been embracing the movie while we've been making it.

What feeling do you want audiences to have?

When we've talked about *Star Wars*, even from the beginning when we were first brought into the process, we really wanted to accomplish creating a film where we could bring back to cinema the experience that we all had decades ago. We want people to return to that experience; it was more than just a movie—it was the whole package and the event and the magic of going to a movie like this that was something really special.

Hopefully, adults who had gone to see *Star Wars* when they were kids will bring their kids to go see it in the theaters and kids will experience something that they can tell their kids about later on. That will be our legacy. When the lights dim, the curtains part and the movie begins, you will be transported to another galaxy far, far away—the same way we all were when we were kids.

Concept art featuring Kylo Ren and his iconic lightsaber. "For me this has been a process where a lot of the external things have been formed that gave me more information," says Adam Driver on Kylo Ren's evolution. "Usually I feel like I try to work internally and try to think about how it feels on the inside out, but for this there are so many tactile things that I can actually hold on to that give me a lot of information. The fight choreography was one of them."

From Concepts to Costumes

MICHAEL KAPLAN WAS CHARGED WITH CREATING THE CLOTHES THAT MAKE THE CHARACTERS IN *THE FORCE AWAKENS*.

HE WHITE GLEAM of a stormtrooper's uniform. Darth Vader's iconic semi-samurai helmet and mask. Leia's bikini, shimmering gold above the Sarlacc pit. The *Star Wars* Universe is jam-packed with memorable characters, all of them decked out in a wondrous wardrobe. So when it came time to find a costume designer for *The Force Awakens*, the film's producers knew they'd need someone who could create lasting looks that both drew from the past and informed the future of the franchise. To meet this challenge, they turned to veteran costume designer Michael Kaplan.

"We've been a fan of Michael Kaplan forever," says producer Bryan Burk. "He began his career with *Blade Runner* and eight gazillion movies since then, so the opportunity to work with him yet again—let alone on something as iconic and personal for all of us—was undeniable." Kaplan and his team worked with J.J. Abrams as well as the actors in many cases to

According to Kylo Ren costume creator Glyn Dillon, the primary inspirations for Kylo Ren's helmet design were the brightly colored stripes on concept artist Chris Foss's 1970s spaceship designs. J.J. Abrams liked the stripes but wasn't sure about them being colored yellow all of the time, so he suggested reflective stripes. The back of Kylo Ren's helmet was an intentional reference to Ralph McQuarrie's classic Darth Vader helmet design.

fully connect the new film's costumes to its characters and their stories while simultaneously nodding to the previous *Star Wars* films. The work speaks for itself. "Michael has done an amazing job," Domhnall Gleeson says. "It absolutely feels like *Star Wars*. You look around, and you immediately know what universe you're in. You wouldn't have to just look at the set because if you look at the costumes, you'd immediately recognize the world. But, it's also slightly different than what they did before."

"The costume was such an evolving thing," says Adam Driver of Kylo Ren's distinctive look. "I'd fly in to see what they were coming up with and the nods—even Kurosawa and his jacket that bows out just a

1. Daisy Ridley on location in Abu Dhabi, a stand-in for the desert planet Jakku. **2.** A concept sketch for Rey showcasing her overall look. **3.** As a scavenger, nearly everything Rey owns has been cobbled together from something originally intended for another purpose. Even her handy staff is built from old parts.

little bit like a samurai—and all those references. Then I'd leave for two weeks and come back to see how it was shaped a little more—such attention to detail." Driver readily admits that Kaplan and co. did most of the work. "My only input was whether it felt good or bad. I was involved in making it functional, which was great. They were all about how they could make it more efficient and something that someone could wear. It looks great, but if you can't move in it or breathe in it, then it doesn't make sense for the audience or the actor."

The costumes weren't the only aspects of each character that had to be contended with. "We went through many versions of hair and a few versions of costume," says Daisy Ridley of Rey's initial look. "When we finally decided on the hair, and I put the costume on, you could feel everyone go, 'That's how she should be.' Everything is supposed to look like Rey put it together herself. So, the hair is the iconic three buns, which we call the three knobs. The costume is gorgeous. It's pretty, but she works in it. Everything she's got fits her perfectly."

Time will tell whether the three knobs will become as recognizably *Star Wars* as Leia's *New Hope* buns, but the hair, the costumes and even the special effects of *The Force Awakens* aren't what producer Kathleen Kennedy thinks people care about. They simply add to what is, overwhelmingly, the thing that makes *Star Wars* so beloved: emotion. "It's about characters; it's about a sense of humor and an emotional response to something," Kennedy says. "It's about people you want to be with."

1

BACK PACK

2

3

FLAME THROWER TROOPER

4

5

1. A concept sketch for a First Order stormtrooper. 2. Conceptual sketch for a snow trooper. 3. A stormtrooper design, updating the look from the original trilogy. 4. A concept sketch for a flame trooper. 5. Original concept art for Captain Phasma. "The costume is absolutely sensational. It is restrictive, but I think it gives us an insight into Captain Phasma," says Gwendoline Christie. "This is a woman who is wearing armor, but her femininity is still displayed. She doesn't try to hide it; it only empowers her further. The costume takes around 45 minutes to put on. It certainly makes me stand up straight. I have a really fantastic pair of boots underneath it all, which I think gives the foundation of Captain Phasma. They're incredibly well made, very stylish, and very hard-wearing—sensible but stylish."

Captain Sidon Ithano, known in some circles as the Crimson Corsair, Blood Buccaneer or Red Raider, is but one of many bizarre denizens of Maz Kanata's castle. This helmet design came from a pool of characters that senior creature sculptor Luke Fisher drew on his computer tablet (inset), which J.J. Abrams subsequently featured in *The Force Awakens*.

A Topix Media Lab Publication
For inquiries, call 646-476-8860

CEO, Co-Founder Tony Romando
Co-Founder Bob Lee
Vice President of Sales and New Markets Tom Mifsud
Vice President of Brand Marketing Joy Bomba
Director of Finance Vandana Patel
Production Manager Nancy Puskuldjian

Editor-in-Chief Jeff Ashworth
Creative Director Steven Charny
Photo Director Dave Weiss
Senior Editor James Ellis
Art Director Elizabeth Neal
Managing Editor Courtney Kerrigan
Associate Editor Tim Baker
Copy Editor Holland Baker
Photo Editor Meg Reinhardt
Assistant Photo Editor Lindsay Pogash
Senior Designer Bryn Waryan
Photo Assistant Kelsey Pillischer
Designer Michelle Lock
Assistant Editors Bailey Bryant, Trevor Courneen, Alicia Kort
Junior Analyst Matthew Quinn
Editorial Assistants Amber Blossman, Sarah Kim, Sophia Noulas
Design Assistant Jansi Buckles

All photos courtesy Lucasfilm

(C) and TM 2015 Lucasfilm LTD.

Kylo Ren ready for battle outside of Maz's castle. "Trying to convey someone whose physical life is very much about combat and fighting in a short amount of time is a challenging thing," Adam Driver says. "One of the first things I wanted to do, as soon as everything was all scheduled, was to get over here as much as possible and start drilling daily and making it part of my daily life."

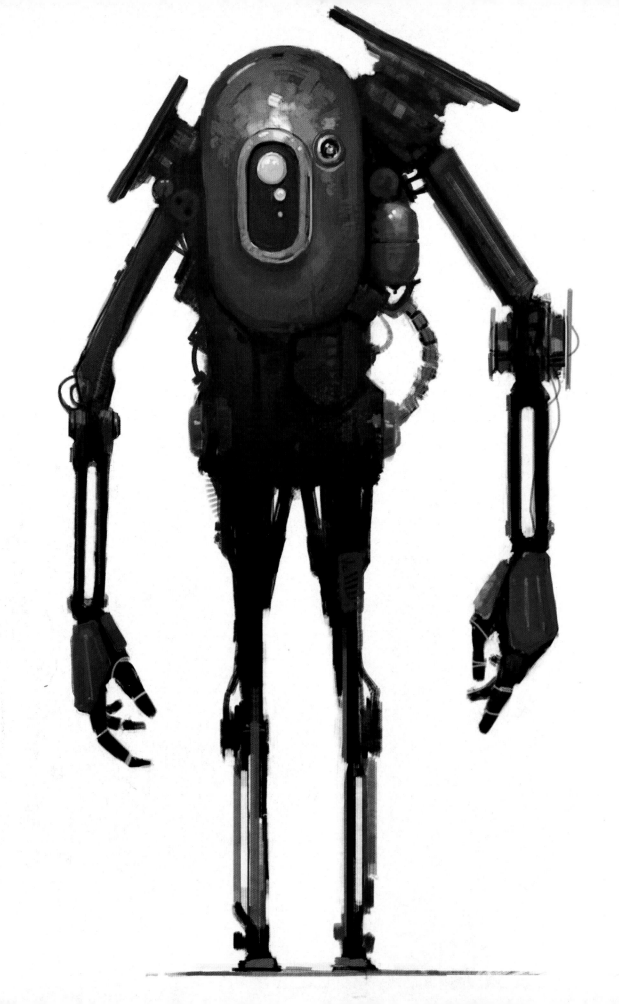

Originally intended for Jakku's Niima Outpost, HURID-327 eventually found a home in the courtyard of Maz Kanata's castle. Senior sculptor Luke Fisher found inspiration in the shape of old tractors for this droid design. Inset: A concept drawing of a Frigosian by Ivan Manzella. Thromba and Laparo, a pair of Frigosian cryptosurgeons, offer reconstructive services to desperate fugitives within the heavy walls of Maz Kanata's castle. The Frigosians were senior creature sculptor Ivan Manzella's throwback to the quirky but charming aliens of science-fiction films and TV series of the 1970s and early '80s such as *Battle Beyond The Stars*. Manzella was also inspired by *The Empire Strikes Back*'s diminutive Ugnaughts of Cloud City.

26/11/13